A SHORT BIOGRAPHY OF MARY LINCOLN

A SHORT BIOGRAPHY OF
Mary Lincoln

Erin Carlson Mast

BENNA BOOKS
Carlisle, Massachusetts

A Short Biography of Mary Lincoln

Series Editor: Susan DeLand
Written by: Erin Carlson Mast

For Andrew

978-1-944038-26-7

Front cover: *Mary Todd Lincoln,* 1925
Katherine Helm
Oil on canvas
32.85 cm x 44.26 cm
White House Collection / White House Historical Association, 165
Back cover: *Lincoln family in 1861*
Painted by F. B. Carpenter; engraved by J. C. Buttre.
Buttre, John Chester, 1821–1893.
Carpenter, F. B. (Francis Bicknell), 1830–1900, artist
New York: J. C. Buttre, 48 Franklin St., c. 1873.
1 print: mezzotint; plate 55.1 cm x 73.2 cm on sheet 61.4 cm x 85.7 cm.
Library of Congress Prints and Photographs Division
Washington, D.C. 20540 USA
2003666395

Published by Benna Books
an imprint of Applewood Books, Inc.
Carlisle, Massachusetts

To request a free copy of our current catalog
featuring our best-selling books, write to:
Applewood Books
P.O. Box 27
Carlisle, Massachusetts 01741
Or visit us on the web at: www.awb.com

10 9 8 7 6 5 4 3 2 1
MANUFACTURED IN THE UNITED STATES OF AMERICA

MARY LINCOLN, FIRST LADY during the United States Civil War, entered this world as Mary Ann Todd on December 13, 1818. She was the fourth of seven children born to Elizabeth and Robert Smith Todd of Lexington, Kentucky.

Mary's ancestors were predominantly of Irish and Scottish descent. David Levi Todd, her paternal great-grandfather, immigrated from Ireland to Kentucky by way of Pennsylvania. Her great-great maternal grandfather, Samuel McDowell, immigrated from Scotland to Pennsylvania.

Mary was born into a family of means. Mary's mother, Elizabeth Ann Todd, née

Parker, married Robert Todd in 1812, the same year he volunteered as an officer in the War of 1812. Eliza, as she was known, ultimately bore seven children, one of whom died before age two.

Eliza never recovered following the birth of her last child, George. Three doctors were summoned in what proved to be a futile effort to save Eliza's life. Mary was only six years old at the time. Within a year, her father remarried. Elizabeth "Betsy" Humphrey, Mary's new stepmother, dramatically changed the dynamic of the Todd household, straining the relationship between Betsy Todd and her husband's children. Mary's father and stepmother ultimately had nine children together, eight of whom survived infancy.

Mary enjoyed an extensive education. Around age eight, she began attending the Shelby Female Academy for lessons in writing, literature, geography, and more. By age fourteen, she was sent to Madame

Despite being raised with the advantages of education, high society, and money, Mary later described her childhood as "desolate."

Mentelle's Boarding School, a finishing school where she added dancing, singing, penmanship, and fluency in French to her skill set. Last, she returned to Shelby, now named Dr. Ward's Academy, where she was exposed to more advanced studies. Mary's education and personality led her contemporaries to note her wit and charm. A Lexington neighbor recalled she was vivacious, but that her wit had a devastating side that could "cut like the sting of a hornet."

Mary originally shared many views in common with her father, including identifying politically as a Whig. Despite denouncing aspects of slavery, however, her father was a wealthy slave owner. Her father's work and family's stature gave Mary direct access to some of the political giants of her time. Her education and exposure to the goings-on of the fledgling democracy planted the seeds for an abiding interest in politics.

Influenced by her admiration of an en-

Henry Clay was a fellow Whig and a neighbor of Mary's in Lexington.

slaved woman in the Todd household, Mammy Sally, and by her maternal grandmother, Mary's antislavery stance grew. Anecdotally, Sally was involved in Underground Railroad efforts, while Mary's grandmother freed some of her own slaves. Mary's education and the new perspectives she gained as she moved from place to place as an adult also shaped her evolving views on what was a singular issue in her time—the incompatibility of slavery and the young nation's founding principles of life, liberty, and the pursuit of happiness.

At age twenty-one, Mary moved to Springfield, Illinois, to live with her eldest sister, Elizabeth, and brother-in-law, Ninian W. Edwards, son of a former governor of Illinois. Mary became part of the social scene in Springfield, attracting the attention of up-and-comer Stephen A. Douglas, a rising star in the Democratic Party, and his future political adversary, Abraham Lincoln, who was a Whig originally from Kentucky.

Aside from Kentucky roots and Whig politics, Mary and Abraham had also both lost their biological mothers at a young age. The similarities ended there. She was a petite five foot two, sophisticated, with coiffed auburn hair and sparkling blue eyes. He was a gangly six foot four, unsophisticated, with unkempt black hair and ten years her senior. He was born in a one-room log cabin, she in a fourteen-bedroom house. And Abraham's schooling, one total year of instruction, was dramatically inferior to Mary's.

According to the most widely accepted story, Mary and Abraham Lincoln met at a dance in December 1839. He said he wanted to dance with her "in the worst way." Mary later joked that he was true to his word, dancing quite literally in the worst way she had witnessed. Nonetheless, Mary was smitten. His affection for her was underscored by giving her the nickname "Molly." Mary's sister and brother-in-law did not approve of what

Though Mary's relationship with her stepmother was stormy, Abraham had great affection for his stepmother.

they considered a mismatch. Compared to some of the other eligible men in town, Abraham lacked sophistication, education, and money. Pressured by their disapproval, he broke off their courtship on the first day of January 1841.

Mary and Abraham avoided one another for over a year until friends brought them together again. Despite their differences, they complemented each other. Their renewed courtship was kept relatively secret. Mary's own sister, Elizabeth, was apparently kept in the dark until the day before the wedding on November 4, 1842. Not only did Elizabeth acquiesce to the marriage, she and Ninian agreed to host the wedding in their house, essentially fulfilling the role typically met by the bride's parents, who did not attend. Even by contemporary standards in Springfield, the nuptials were private and hurried— etiquette dictated at least one week's notice.

Abraham referred to the day his courtship with Mary was broken off as "the fatal first of January."

Mary and Abraham's first home together was a single room at the Globe Tavern, a boardinghouse and a dramatic departure from Mary's expansive childhood home or the beautiful house in which she had been living with her sister. In that one-room apartment Mary gave birth to their first child, Robert "Bob" Todd Lincoln, on August 1, 1843. Later they moved into the first and only house they would ever own, a one-and-a-half-story house on the corner of Eighth and Jackson Streets. They eventually expanded the house to two stories and lived there for seventeen years. In their new home, Mary gave birth to their second son, Edward "Eddie" Baker Lincoln, on March 10, 1846.

The Lincolns' room at the Globe Tavern measured eight by fourteen feet.

Abraham never attended law school. The only requirement to practice law was to obtain a certificate from an Illinois county court certifying good moral character. As a circuit lawyer, Abraham was frequently absent, leaving Mary alone with the children, occasionally joined by a relative or hired domestic servant.

In 1846 life changed dramatically. Abraham Lincoln was elected to the United States House of Representatives and began his term on March 4, 1847. Mary made the atypical move of relocating with her husband to the nation's capital, Washington, D.C. Her husband's election to national office demonstrated that she had been right about his potential all along and that her efforts on his behalf had not been in vain.

In Washington, the family lived in Mrs. Sprigg's boardinghouse, along with several abolitionist congressmen.

> "I would rather marry a good man—a man of mind—with a hope and bright prospects ahead for position—fame & power than to marry all the houses gold & bones in the world."

On their journey east, the Lincolns made several stops to see friends and family along the way, including a visit to Lexington, Kentucky. Mary returned triumphantly, the wife of an elected U.S. representative and mother of two spirited boys. During their month-long stay, Mary and Abe developed a strong relationship with Mary's eleven-year-old half-sister, Emilie, whom they called "Little Sister." The Lincolns arrived in Washington in early December of 1847. Mary's triumph quickly turned to frustration. In Springfield, she was known as an astute hostess. In Washington, she was a virtual nobody, despite being a distant relation of Dolley Madison, widow of former president James Madison. Dolley still commanded considerable social and political respect in Washington, having been the First Lady against whom all others were measured.

Mary eventually left with little Robert and Eddie, staying with family in Lexington. That spring, Lincoln wrote to her, noting that while he thought her and the

While separated, Mary teased her husband that little Eddie may have forgotten him.

boys' presence "hindered" him in his work, he was missing them dearly. At one point, Mary noted that she was surprisingly free of migraines, which plagued her most of her adult life. Abraham responded with something close to delighted surprise. Their correspondence demonstrates a comfortable, loving relationship.

Mary and the boys reunited with Abraham by the end of his term. Prior to returning to Springfield, the Lincolns actively engaged in the 1848 presidential election, throwing their support behind Whig candidate Zachary Taylor. At the time, presidential candidates did not campaign for themselves; rather, others did so on their behalf. And many who campaigned on the behalf of the winning candidate often sought political appointments. The Lincolns were no different.

Mary took the task of writing letters to Whig leaders, seeking a position for her husband. Abraham, passed over for more

The Lincolns' dear friend Edward Baker, for whom their second child was named, moved to the Pacific Northwest and became one of the first U.S. senators from Oregon.

prestigious and desirable appointments, was offered the position of governor of the Oregon territory. Mary persuaded her husband to decline the offer. It was a political dead-end for the Lincolns: Oregon was a Democrat stronghold and offered comparatively little power. Furthermore, moving to the vast frontier territory would have taken Mary and her family that much farther away from relations and close friends.

In 1849 the Lincolns returned to Springfield and slipped back into their roles in the household and community. Tragedy struck again. Eddie, their tender-hearted second son, died, a month shy of his fourth birthday. The parents were devastated by the loss. They carried on in spite of their grief, and at the end of the year welcomed their third son, William "Willie" Wallace Lincoln. Three years later, their fourth son, Thomas "Tad" Lincoln, was born. Adding to their own family, the

The Lincoln boys were known for being rambunctious, with one observing they were "notorious hellions" with permissive parents.

Lincolns welcomed "Little Sister" Emilie Todd to stay with them the following year.

Mary had a legendarily preoccupied husband, and it is during this time in their lives that most of the recollections of Mary flying into a fury or berating her husband surface. In one such incident, Mary discovered one of their children crying on the ground, her husband obliviously pushing an empty baby carriage.

Despite the daily stresses, their prospects were improving. Abraham's burgeoning legal career and the sale of farmland they received from Mary's father gave them the resources to expand and properly appoint their home. There was a considerable setback when the house caught fire. According to recollections, Mary and Emilie were attending a party when Mary became insistent they return home. They did so only to find the house ablaze, the children inside, and their caretaker asleep. Thankfully, the children were saved.

Some time later, a lightning bolt caused a second fire to the Lincoln home, burning part of the roof.

During this time, too, the Whig Party was crumbling and the new Republican Party was forming, with the issue of slavery central to its platform. The Lincolns saw an opportunity with the presidential election of 1860. Mary successfully helped make her husband the Republican candidate. Veteran politicians and journalists came west to meet the upstart candidate. The Lincolns were under the magnifying glass. Mary fulfilled her role with aplomb. The press lauded her for being amiable and accomplished. By this time, their oldest son, Robert, was at school in the East. Mary missed him terribly. While she kept up the appearance of a gracious hostess, the campaign also took its toll.

In an election with four major candidates, Abraham Lincoln won the presidency. Victory must have tasted especially sweet for Mary. She was an incredibly ambitious woman, but like most women of her time, her fate was tied directly to the fate of her

Though Illinois went for Abraham Lincoln, their home state of Kentucky did not.

husband. Mary may have looked forward to an even more triumphant journey east, this time as the wife of the president-elect of the United States of America. But if her personal ambition was to mirror or exceed the achievements of a Dolley Madison, that dream was painfully dashed.

Southern states began seceding in the months leading up to Abraham Lincoln's inauguration. By the time the Lincolns arrived in Washington, D.C., seven states had left the Union and tensions were high. Washington was very much a Southern city at the time. Rather than sweeping into the nation's capital victorious, Mary found herself in the middle of a social and political minefield.

Mary's first major appearance in Washington was the Inaugural Ball. She was praised for her grace and poise by many, and the event was deemed a success. There was, however, a sizable contingent that boycotted the affair entirely. In the weeks after the Inaugural Ball, it was plain to observers that Mary Lincoln was being snubbed.

That summer, the Lincolns intended to relocate from the Executive Mansion, as the White House was then known, to a cottage located three miles north, on the grounds of the Old Soldiers Home. The location was one of the highest points in Washington, D.C., and considered a healthier location than the Executive Mansion, which was in a marshy, low-lying part of the city. James Buchanan, Lincoln's predecessor, had lived there for part of his summers in office and had written to his niece that he slept much more comfortably there than at the Executive Mansion. Before this move could be made, however, Fort Sumter was attacked. The Civil War had begun.

While her husband threw himself into his dual role of president of the United States and commander in chief of the

Mary returned the snubs by avoiding events such as social rival Kate Chase's 1863 wedding, dubbed the social event of the season.

Union Army, Mary did what she could to fulfill her duties. In so doing, she found herself in no-win situations. She was criticized for the shabby condition of the Executive Mansion, then criticized for her redecorating expenses during the horrific war. Her missteps were highlighted; her good deeds went unnoticed. There was considerable attention paid to Mary's spending habits, while few knew of her visits to nearby army hospitals during the war. She brought the sick and wounded soldiers fruit, to comfort them, and wrote messages home on their behalf.

She was also active in supporting the Contraband Relief Association, which provided food, supplies, and money to formerly enslaved people. The organization was cofounded by Elizabeth Keckly, herself a former slave. After arriving in Washington, Mary hired Keckly to make dresses for her, and they became confidants. When emancipation came to the District in April 1862, men, women, and children fled to freedom in the District, resulting in a refugee crisis. Keckly addressed the needs of the refugees, and Mary heeded her call. She beseeched her husband to make a $200 donation to the association, the single largest donation made that year.

Keckly also was at Mary's side when she needed her most. In the midst of national tragedy, the Lincolns were struck time and again with personal tragedy. Their dear friend Elmer Ellsworth was the first official Union death in the Civil War. Then, in February 1862, Willie fell ill. Mary wanted to cancel a large ball that had been planned at the White House. The event continued when the doctor assured the Lincolns that Willie was in "no immediate danger." Throughout the night, the nervous parents checked in on Willie, to whom Keckly and others tended. Then Tad, too, fell ill. A great cloud of despair hung over the family.

Willie and Tad Lincoln likely contracted typhoid fever from contaminated drinking water.

Willie Lincoln died at the age of eleven on February 20, 1862. Mary was plunged into an all-consuming grief with their loss of a second child. Tad, thankfully, made a full recovery from his illness but was devastated by the loss of his constant companion. Mary found the sight of Tad's playmates too difficult and kept them away. Abraham and Robert were distraught but worked to contain their emotions. According to Keckly, Abraham, fearing for his wife's sanity, told Mary that if she did not improve, he would have to send her to St. Elizabeth's, a mental hospital visible from the Executive Mansion.

While the Lincolns were in the depths of personal despair, the Union enjoyed a string of much-needed victories. Mary found the celebratory military drills and musical concerts too much to bear. In the summer of 1862, the Lincolns moved to a cottage at the Soldiers Home in the northern part of the District. Writing to a friend, Mary explained that in their sorrow, quiet was necessary to them. Mary was pleased with their move.

The Soldiers Home provided no retreat from tragedy. The nation's first home for disabled veteran soldiers was perched on a strategically important hilltop. Living there gave the Lincolns a front-row seat to the human cost of war. Their immediate neighbors were 100–200 disabled veterans. The daily commute into the city brought them into close contact with caravans of wounded soldiers and refugees. In their first year, over a thousand soldiers were buried a couple hundred yards away in the Soldiers Home National Cemetery, the predecessor of Arlington National Cemetery.

While Kentucky remained within the Union, several Todd family members fought for the Confederacy. The hardest of these to take was Benjamin Hardin Helm, husband to Emilie, their dear "Lit-

> "We are truly delighted, with this retreat, the drives & walks around here are delightful, & each day, brings its visitors."

The husband of Mary's favorite half-sister served as a Confederate general and was killed at the Battle of Chickamauga.

tle Sister." Benjamin refused President Lincoln's offer to become a U.S. Army paymaster and became a Confederate general instead. When Benjamin died, the Lincolns invited Emilie to come stay with them. Hosting a Confederate widow fueled unfounded aspersions that Mary was a Confederate sympathizer or even a spy. She may have felt grief for the loss of family fighting and dying for the Confederacy, but she was resolute in the Union cause.

> *"They would kill my husband if they could, and destroy our government—the dearest of all things to us."*

Although she was a devout Protestant, Mary also became involved in "spirit circles." Spiritualism was a growing movement that exploded in popularity during the war, fueled by the mass suffering and casualties. Séances seemed to offer Mary and many families what they wanted most—a means of connecting with their departed loved ones. Abraham, ever the skeptic, became concerned that his wife was falling victim to con artists and requested that reporter Noah Brooks attend a séance at the Lincolns' cottage at the Soldiers Home. The medium, the self-styled Lord Colchester, was caught in the act of faking spirit communication. He threatened blackmail. The incident was a great embarrassment.

As war waged, Mary spent more time away from Washington. She made trips to New York and parts of New England, taking Tad with her. They visited Robert at Harvard, went on shopping excursions, and went to the White Mountains of New Hampshire. These trips appear to have done little to ease her depression and severe migraines, which became more frequent after she suffered a serious head injury from a carriage accident between the Soldiers Home and the Executive Mansion.

Although there were legitimate reasons for Mary to venture north for her health, her shopping on these trips was a source of public criticism. Her husband, focused on the war, seemed ignorant of his wife's mounting debts. Mary became increasingly concerned about what might happen if her husband failed to win reelection in 1864. In a conversation with Keckly, Mary said: "The President glances at my rich dresses and is happy to believe that the few hundred dollars that I obtain from him supply all my wants. If he is elected, I can keep him in ignorance of my affairs, but if he is defeated, then the bills will be sent."

Fortunately for Mary and the nation, President Lincoln was reelected in 1864. Six months later the Confederacy surrendered. The change in national mood was

In the summer of 1864, Mary, Robert, and Tad visited the Equinox House, a hotel and spa in the foothills of the Green Mountains.

palpable. On April 13, 1865, the Lincolns went on a carriage ride to the Soldiers Home and spoke of better times ahead, but joy was painfully short-lived.

The very next night, the Lincolns attended a comedy, *Our American Cousin,* at Ford's Theatre. Mary and Abraham held hands as they enjoyed the play with their guests, Clara Harris and Major Henry Rathbone, in the presidential box. Mary whispered to her husband, "What will Miss Harris think of my hanging on to you so?" The president reportedly replied and said with a smile, "She won't think anything about it." Abraham Lincoln was shot in the head by John Wilkes Booth moments later. Mary was still holding her husband's hand.

The attack was part of a coordinated effort to eliminate the Union leadership. In the immediate aftermath, Abraham was carried to the Petersen boardinghouse across the street. Mary, in hysterics, accompanied her wounded husband as he was laid out on a bed. Secretary of War Edwin Stanton forced her to be removed from the room and returned to the Executive Mansion. Their eldest son, Robert, was summoned and would stay with his father throughout the night. The following morning, President Lincoln died.

In the days that followed, Mary let others take care of all arrangements including the funeral and public viewing in the East Room of the White House. On April 21, 1865, the remains of Abraham and Willie Lincoln, whose casket was exhumed, began the long trip back to Springfield, Illinois, by train. While five friends and family accompanied the funeral train, Mary and her two surviving sons did not. Her husband's death caused an outpouring of public support. One notable letter Mary received was from Queen Victoria, who had lost her husband several years earlier. Mary replied:

"I have received the letter which Your Majesty has had the kindness to write. I am deeply grateful for this expression of tender sympathy, coming as they do, from a heart which from its own sorrow, can appreciate the intense grief I now endure."

Mary remained in the Executive Mansion until May 23, 1865, when she and Tad moved to Chicago, where she began an unending battle over her husband's legacy and a pension. She was humiliated publicly by William Herndon, her husband's former law partner, who went on the lecture circuit in 1866 suggesting the Lincolns had a loveless marriage. Herndon and Mrs. Lincoln had never had an amicable relationship, and his public statements about their private life made him an enemy of the Lincoln family.

Financially, Mary was frustrated that her husband's former colleagues achieved

Mary gave many of her husband's belongings away as mementos. Other people simply helped themselves, even cutting out bits of the White House draperies.

In 1867, she wrote: "I feel assured his watchful, loving eyes are always watching over us, and he is fully aware of the wrong and injustice permitted his family by a country he lost his life in protecting."

wealth and prominence thanks to her husband's presidency, while she was left to fend for herself. She battled Congress over the pension she felt the nation owed her as it did other war widows.

In her desperation, she became involved in a scheme that became known as the "Old Clothes Scandal." She connected with brokers in New York who agreed to sell her clothing and personal effects. The brokers convinced her to do this publicly and to pen letters about her poverty and the Republicans she had helped who were now turning their backs on her. The brokers planned essentially to blackmail prominent Republicans into delivering funds to avoid the public sale and publication of the letters in a Democrat newspaper. The scheme backfired, and Mary was vilified by the public, Republican Party officials, and Robert, who was mortified by his mother's actions. In 1868, she moved to Germany with Tad.

Mary did not return to the United States

Sixteen years later, Mary's pension was increased by Congress, due in large part to it granting President Garfield's widow a more generous pension after his assassination.

until 1871. Tragedy struck yet again when Tad fell ill and died that same year, at the age of eighteen. In the ensuing years, Mary's behavior became so alarming and embarrassing to her remaining son, Robert, that he had her tried for insanity. Robert believed that money issues were the root cause of Mary's mania. He won the case and had her committed to Bellevue Insane Asylum in Batavia, Illinois. Mary felt utterly betrayed by her only remaining son.

Mary appealed the decision and her case was taken up by attorney Myra Bradwell, who was convinced Mary was committed under false pretenses. She won and Mary was released to the care of her sister Elizabeth in Springfield. A second trial in 1876 established her sanity, and Mary moved to Pau, France. During this time, her health continued to decline. On top of her severe headaches, she began suffering from damaging cataracts, and spinal cord injuries from a fall in 1879.

Myra Bradwell was one of the nation's first female lawyers.

Mary returned to her sister Elizabeth's home in 1880. On July 16, 1882, she fell into a coma. Mary died later that day at the age of sixty-three. Her remains were buried alongside her husband's in the family tomb in Oak Ridge Cemetery in Springfield.

Long after her death, Mary's life has continued to generate intense interest and scrutiny, as well as new scholarship. In the 1990s and early 2000s, for example, researchers found files—which most had assumed were long since destroyed—on Mary Lincoln's insanity trials. The files provided new context for what transpired, including her family's views on her institutionalization, a psychiatric account of Mary's mental state, and correspondence with her attorney on how she would get released. The discovery was a reminder that there is always more to the story, and more to the legacy of memorable First Lady Mary Lincoln.